SOME SHORTISE
for the Sundays in Ordinary Time
Year A

GLORIFYING
THE LORD
BY YOUR LIFE

James O'Kane

Acknowledgment

Use has been made throughout of the English version of Volume I of the Roman Lectionary approved for use in Ireland in 1981.

The Homilist

Father James O'Kane was born in Belfast where he received his earliest education from Dominican Sisters and at Christian Brothers' schools. After seminary formation in Belfast and Rome he undertook postgraduate studies at Louvain and was ordained in 1976. From 1979 he taught spiritual and moral theology at Maynooth. Since 1995 he has served in Newtownards & Comber, Ballintoy & Ballinlea, Culfeightrin, Kilcoo and Cushendun & Torr.

Second Sunday

Here I am, Lord! I come to do your will.

This is a courageous prayer, brothers and sisters in Christ. For we can never be sure what God's will for us is going to be. We can look back, of course, and be quietly confident that all that has happened to us already has somehow been God's will for us, our preparation for this present moment and all that is yet to come. Although even that is not always easy. It is no straightforward thing simply to accept all that has been and to accept it as coming from God for our good.

Here I am, Lord. I come to do your will. It is a prayer too of freedom. It says that we are ready at last to go along with God. It says that we have begun to realise that we too have our own little place in the great plan. But we come slowly to this conviction. It is something that dawns on us over the years of our life. Often when we look back over our story we have the humbling experience of seeing that the really special things that happened through us were not our doing at all. God works through us, often despite our best efforts to do something else. Often what our lives were really about when we look back over them was something quite different from whatever it was we thought important at the time.

Here I am, Lord. I come to do your will. It is a prayer too of hope at those strange times in our lives when we are no longer too sure who we are and cannot make sense of where we have ended up. Yes, a courageous prayer, a prayer of freedom, a prayer of hope, that does not ask to know the future. It is enough, it has to be enough, this confidence of faith, that in his will is our peace.

And that is why every individual person is so important and precious, each one formed in his or her mother's womb to be God's servant, so that light may triumph over darkness in our human world and salvation reach to the ends of the earth. We all have our own little place in the great plan. We are all called out of the dreary isolation of sin - for yes, that is what sin is, the dreariest isolation of all - and we are called, as Saint Paul puts it, to take our place among all the saints everywhere who pray to our Lord Jesus Christ and so become his holy people.

Here I am, Lord. I come to do your will. John the Baptist, in his complete lack of self-importance, is a splendid example of this prayer lived with sincerity. His consciousness that the meaning of his life was to prepare the way for Jesus makes him profoundly Christian. We too, when we are at our most Christian, are preparing the way for Jesus - in our hearts and in our lives, in our families and in our work, in our community and in our world. For Jesus is the lamb of God that takes away the sin of the world, Jesus is the chosen one of God who comes to baptise us with the Holy Spirit.

The danger is that we grow deaf to God, that we lose our sense of sin, that we forget the Holy Spirit given to us in Baptism. Here I am, Lord. I come to do your will. It is a courageous prayer, a prayer of freedom, a prayer of hope, that promises God an open ear and expresses our longing for his peace in us and around us.

Isaiah 49:4.5-6 / First Corinthians 1:1-3 / John 1:29-34

Third Sunday

The people that walked in darkness has seen a great light; on those who live in a land of deep shadow a light has shone.

This prophecy of Isaiah that Matthew sees fulfilled in Jesus, brothers and sisters in Christ, is rich in promise for all of us. All of us, in one way or another, know what it is to walk in darkness, to live in a land of deep shadow. Often children, and not only children, are afraid of the dark. This does not mean that a light in the darkness is always reassuring in a straightforward way. We do not know what we will see when the light goes on. Perhaps it will illumine familiar and safe surroundings - but what if it merely reveals a path into the unknown and a compelling invitation to follow that path at the expense of all that is familiar and safe?

The message of Jesus is urgent: Repent! - for the kingdom of heaven is close at hand. His approach to individual men and women is direct and unambiguous. Follow me, is his call to the brothers Simon and Andrew, and James and John and at once, we are told, at once, they followed him. At once.

There is no suggestion that these men, these first disciples now known to us as four of the twelve apostles, there is no suggestion that they were consciously unhappy with their lives as they were. They were fishermen - and their trade and their families would have provided them with as much material and emotional security as any of us might wish for. Indeed for those who see their religion as an extra bit of insurance - just in case - it must be quite a shock to realise that Jesus calls his disciples away from precisely those things that we all cling on to, and at times cling on to with a certain desperation.

They left their nets at once and followed him. Simon and Andrew leave their past and their security behind and embark upon the adventure to which they are called. Follow me and I will make you fishers of men, Jesus told them. James and

John too, at once, leaving the boat and their father followed him. They turn their backs on all that has been dear to them and the very substance of their lives, rich with its own promises and hopes for their futures, and they move on - into the freedom to which Jesus invites them.

Repent, for the kingdom of heaven is close at hand. This is the light that Jesus comes to shed upon the darkness of our lives. If we do not hear his call it could be that, so far from being afraid of the dark, we have actually made ourselves comfortable, all too comfortable, in our darkness. We have pulled down the blinds, drawn the curtains and locked the doors. We are comfortable in our darkness and we fear the light.

Jesus came to Simon and Andrew, James and John in their everyday world, Follow me, he urged them as he freed them from the shackles of their past, the chains of their securities, the entanglements of their attachments. He changed their lives forever. He wants to do the same for us. Today. At once. Let us not stand in his way. Let us allow him to draw us out of our darkness - no matter how painful that may be, for that pain is our cross. Jesus urges us to follow him, through the cross into resurrection and life. Let us allow him to draw us out of our darkness into the glory of his own wonderful light where we will find freedom and joy and peace.

Isaiah 8:23 – 9:3 / First Corinthians 1:10-13.17 / Matthew 4:12-23

Fourth Sunday

This is what he taught them.

We have all heard the beatitudes before, brothers and sisters in Christ. Perhaps we hear a word in them that speaks to our own poverty, suffering and need. Or perhaps they shock us a little, challenge us and threaten us, because we glimpse that our own lives are about something else, solidly rooted in other principles. Just when we are waiting to be congratulated on doing so well despite every kind of difficulty they seem to hint that life and truth are waiting for us in precisely those difficulties and that it is what we so cheerfully think of as success that is really an aberration. In the end, not to find ourselves fully in the beatitudes is to know our failure in discipleship, for they are Jesus' description of what it would be like for us to live as he did. It is only when we have prayed these beat-itudes on our knees with tears in our eyes that our lives open to God and begin to be transformed in the cross and resurrection of Jesus.

Perhaps each one of us needs to take just one of the beatitudes, perhaps the one that jumped out at us just now when we heard them read to us or the one that strikes us as we cast an eye over them again. Do it now, if you feel able to. Take one of the beatitudes and make it your own. Plant it in your mind and heart. And keep it with you today and everyday until it has changed your life and set you free.

Jesus says: How happy are the poor in spirit. But we envy the rich, strive to succeed and, when all else fails, do our best to hide our poverty, our suffering and our need.

Jesus says: Happy the gentle. But we despise them, admiring instead those who are on permanent alert and ready to fight.

Jesus says: Happy those who mourn. But we have learnt not to show our emotions, to smile all day long or at least practise a stiff upper lip when we are out and about.

Jesus says: Happy are those who

hunger and thirst for what is right. But we are happy to settle for the little things we do for God and leave our comfortable compromises in place.

Jesus says: Happy the merciful. But we would prefer to see justice done and find revenge the sweetest thing of all

.

Jesus says: Happy the pure in heart. But we can barely glimpse what that might mean for us.

Jesus says: Happy the peacemakers. But we find the price too high, the willingness to die sooner than damage another human being.

Jesus says: Happy those who are persecuted in the cause of right. And that we are happy to agree with, for it sounds like a self-satisfaction we could understand and, besides, we are sure we are clever enough to find an easier way of putting things right in the world.

God help us all to see with the eyes of Jesus and begin to understand ourselves and our world with his mind and heart.

To have grasped that there really is no other way is to begin to hope.

Zephaniah 2:3; 3:12-13 / First Corinthians 1:26-31 / Matthew 5:1-12

Fifth Sunday

You are the salt of the earth ... You are the light of the world.

Challenging words these, brothers and sisters in Christ, and, in their own way, encouraging. You are the salt of the earth. You are the light of the world. Do we have a sense of pride in hearing these words again, or do they not leave us feeling uneasy? Are they reason for self-satisfaction, or simply a sad reminder of what might have been?

You are the salt of the earth. You are the light of the world. The first disciples heard these words with a different ear. We remember who they were, people of little account as the world judges such things whom Jesus had rescued from sickness and despair, people crushed by life and shadowed by death whom Jesus had awoken to a new faith and confidence in God as their Father. They knew that they were called to be the salt of the earth and the light of the world by sharing this awareness with others, by widening the circle of the family of God to reach out and embrace the whole of humankind.

You are the salt of the earth. You are the light of the world. We are judged by these words and much about us is condemned by them. But that is not their chief purpose. They are an invitation to renewal. They invite us to re-assess our personal situation and make a new beginning. They tell us that however dreary and insipid we have allowed our lives to be-come, that need not be the last word about us.

We can remember that the Spirit of God has been poured out upon us making us his children and in that remembrance we have a new sense of who we are called to be. We leave the past behind and move into a new future of hope and confidence - and the miracle of this conversion is that we draw others with us because, quite simply, as Jesus puts it, a city built on a hill-top cannot be hidden, a light on a lamp stand shines for everyone in the house. All too often we cast a shadow over those around us. Jesus invites us instead to bring light and joy to all we meet and not least to those who are closest to us. Your light must shine in the sight of men, so that seeing your good works they may give praise to your Father in heaven.

You are the salt of the earth. You are the light of the world. Of course initially, in our early encounters with him, Jesus presses us to focus on our own personal predicament. But the real force of these words of challenge and encouragement is that they are addressed to us together, as a group, as a group of disciples. More specifically they are addressed to us as Church. More specifically still they are addressed to us as Parish. We are called, together, to be salt to this community where we are at home, to be light to all the various little worlds we inhabit, the little worlds where we live and work and play, the little worlds in which we commit ourselves to becoming more fully the salt of the earth and the light of the world at this time and in this place that are so uniquely our own.

Glorifying the Lord by Your Life

Isaiah 58:7-10 / First Corinthians 2:1-5 / Matthew 5:13-16

Sixth Sunday

For I tell you, if your virtue goes no deeper than that of the scribes and Pharisees, you will never get into the kingdom of heaven.

This is an unsettling statement, brothers and sisters in Christ. Jesus is telling us to get real. Simple statement of fact: If your virtue goes no deeper than that of the scribes and Pharisees, you will never get into the kingdom of heaven.

The virtue of the scribe in every generation is to have at his fingertips all the best theories about right and wrong and how to live a good moral life. The virtue of the Pharisee in every generation is his commitment to keeping the rules, and being seen to keep them. Jesus finds them wanting, the scribes and Pharisees of every time and place, sad victims of their own virtue.

No doubt the world would be a better place without murder, adultery, perjury and the like. But we have no grounds for self-satisfaction just because we ourselves have thus far managed to get by without them. Jesus insists that we look into our hearts. It takes courage to do that. At first, by the very nature of things, we will not see very much. But as the eyes of our mind adjust to that inner darkness we can begin to acknowledge our demons. We may well identify within us an anger, or a lust, or a denial of reality, a demon that assumes illusive shapes and seeks devious satisfactions.

Such things may not perhaps, thus far at least, have troubled the smugness and respectability of our outward shell but they rise at times too close for comfort to the surface of our lives. We don't need to read the Sunday papers or surf the internet to know that situations develop in which ordinary and seemingly normal people drift into dishonesty, or sexual misconduct, or violence as the only way for them to get what they want.

If you wish, you can keep the commandments, the Old Testament Wisdom assures us in today's first reading. To behave faithfully is within your power. We too easily make excuses for ourselves. We'd like to forget just how responsible we are for the choices we make, the little everyday choices as much as the big once-in-a-lifetime choices. Man has life and death before him, that Old Testament reading reminds us, whichever a man likes better will be given him. We make our own choices and we have to live with the consequences. There is no choice about consequences. Every choice we make has consequences for ourselves and for others, consequences for better or for worse, once and for all.

Jesus demands more, not less, of his disciples. He asks us to discipline our thoughts and emotions and reject every compromise no matter how high the price. In his death on the cross he has shown us that no price is too high for the freedom and life he has won for us in the glory of his resurrection.

This is a wisdom, Saint Paul reminds us, that none of the masters of this age has ever known, or they would not have crucified the Lord of Glory: the things that no eye has seen and no ear has heard, things beyond the human mind, all that God has prepared for those who love him.

These are the very things that God has revealed to us through the Spirit, for the Spirit reaches the depths of everything, the depths of the human heart and the depths of God himself, offering us a new moral depth beyond the imagined certainties of scribe and Pharisee, the moral depth of full and definitive citizenship in the kingdom of heaven.

Ecclesiasticus 15:15-20 / First Corinthians 2:6-10 / Matthew 5:17-37

Seventh Sunday

You have learnt how it was said: Eye for eye and tooth for tooth. But I say this to you: offer the wicked man no resistance.

A difficult gospel, brothers and sisters in Christ, that has not made much progress. Eye for eye and tooth for tooth - the Jewish law of retaliation has perhaps been refined but it has not been generally superseded in the way Jesus intended. Are we not ever ready to demand our rights? Are we not constantly primed to hit back? Have we not even developed a provocative way of turning the other cheek that invites a slap in the face?

But I say this to you: offer the wicked man no resistance. The Christian response to violence is gentleness. And it can be extremely effective. When we turn the other cheek in a gentle way we afford our attacker the opportunity to reflect on what he is doing: he has struck once in a moment of thoughtless violence does he really want to strike again? If a man takes you to law and would have your tunic, let him have your cloak as well. It is an act of kindness and kindness heals. When others share with us what we need we learn that sharing makes us human. Our grasping selfishness drags us down and cuts us off from others and leads us into an unending spiral of violence. And if anyone orders you to go one mile, go two miles with him. Generosity teaches us that there is no need to command and bully. Where others genuinely care it is enough to ask for what we need. And the converse is true too. To see someone's need and do nothing is already to have refused their cry for help.

The Christian understands violence as a cry for help and responds with gentleness. Jesus suggests that when we do this we show ourselves to be true children of our Father in heaven who causes his sun to rise on the bad as well as the good, and his rain to fall on honest and dishonest people alike. Evil will be overcome by good or not at all. Two wrongs never make a right. Two wrongs make three and four and five and so on for ever. Jesus died on the cross so that his disciples might deliver this message to the world and the world has no answer to such compassion and goodness and love.

Leviticus 19:1-2.17-18 / First Corinthians 3:16-23 / Matthew 5:38-48

Eighth Sunday

So do not worry. Do not say: What are we to eat? What are we to drink? How are we to be clothed? It is the pagans who set their hearts on all these things. Your heavenly Father knows you need them all.

Many of us who are that bit older, brothers and sisters in Christ, grew up in a largely Catholic environment. Or so at least we thought at the time. Now we find ourselves in a very different world, and begin to wonder about our Catholic past. It all looks a bit shallow now in the cold light of the twenty-first century. Certainly our ancestors held on to the ancient faith through several generations of persecution and poverty but that rich heritage has not been honoured in the onward march of history with its new freedoms and its material prosperity.

We are suddenly waking up, so to speak, in a very different world. The land of saints and scholars has vanished into the mists of time. The sustaining graces of persecution and simplicity of life are no more. We are waking up to a very different world. A pagan world. A world where being a Christian is more complicated, and requires more conviction and more commitment. The pagans around us are often pleasant enough people. They're entertaining to watch and fun to be with, especially when they're getting plenty of what they want. The only pagans we might need to feel a little sorry for are the more recent converts who imagine that they are still Catholics, that they can, so to speak, have their cake and eat it. No one can be the slave of two masters: he will either hate the first and love the second, or treat the first with respect and the second with scorn.

We cannot expect to serve the God and Father of our Lord Jesus Christ and still somehow keep in with one or other of the old pagan gods who have never gone away and have now re-emerged in such attractive and fashionable garb in our own times. That is why I am telling you, says Jesus still to anyone who will listen to him, that is why I am telling you not to worry about your life, and what you are to eat or drink, nor about your body, how you look, and what to wear. It is the pagans who set their hearts on such things. The more world-weary pagans, I imagine, would be only too glad to hear such a message and embrace it if only they could. What a relief that would be. Your heavenly Father knows what you need, and better than you do yourselves. Set your hearts on his kingdom first, and on his righteousness, and everything else will be given to you as well. Do not worry about tomorrow: tomorrow will take care of itself. Each day has enough trouble of its own.

Each day has enough trouble of its own. It is for each one of us to know whether or not we will today seize hold of the gift of faith that is offered to us afresh and make our own the vision of life that goes with it. The challenge is that we, each of us, have the freedom to do exactly as we please and to go our own way. It is only at the end that the secrets of our hearts will be revealed and each of us receive whatever we deserve from God.

Sundays in Ordinary Time – Year A

Isaiah 49:14-15 / First Corinthians 4:1-5 / Matthew 6:24-34

Ninth Sunday

Everyone who listens to these words of mine and does not act on them will be like a stupid man who built his house on sand.

There are times, brothers and sisters in Christ, when our failure to build our house on the solid rock of faith in Jesus begins to catch up with us and cracks appear in structures we had put in place to shelter and sustain us.

Of course the words Jesus is referring to are his whole message about life, his words of life, specifically the three chapters of Matthew's Gospel to which the tradition has given the collective name of the Sermon on the Mount and which have been read to us over these last six Sundays. But it is instructive enough for us to start with the words of this Sunday's extract: It is not those who say to me Lord, Lord who will enter the kingdom of heaven, but the person who does the will of my Father in heaven. At the end it will not be enough to have had all the right words. It will not be enough to have been part of some or even all of the right things. Jesus will be waiting for us to tell us to our faces: I have never known you; away from me, you evil people.

There must be some terrible point here that we have missed - not only those of us who feel we need a little bit of religion in our lives to help us through, but even those of us who take religion really seriously and mean to give it a large place in our lives, even at some personal inconvenience. Apparently we have all built on sand and when rain comes and floods rise and gales blow and hurl themselves against our house, there can be only the one outcome, as inevitable as it is disappointing. Our house will fall.

To build our house on the solid rock of faith in Jesus is something different. It is the effective doing of the will of our Father in heaven. The one true God is, after all, a jealous God. He asks for our total commitment. There can be no place in our lives for the false gods of paganism.

We have the same choice Moses set before the people of Israel after he led them away from the slavery of Egypt. The same awesome choice between blessing and curse. What is wrong with us that we choose again and again the curse of disobedience? We talk much too dismissively of the false gods of paganism as if they didn't exist. The false gods of paganism are as real as the most attractive things in all the world. They are the most beautiful things around us. They are false only in the sense that they are not God, they are not divine. They are God's gift to his creation. They become God's enemies only when we allow them to ensnare and enslave us - and, quite literally, lead us away from the one true God.

Saint Paul describes the human predicament in dramatic terms: Both Jew and pagan, he insists, sinned and forfeited God's glory. We have all sinned and fallen short of the glory of God. The mission of Jesus is to make things right again - to make things right between humanity and their God. This reconciliation between us and God is a free gift of grace that becomes real for us as we make our own the redemption worked for us by Jesus on the cross. This is the rock of our faith upon which we can safely build. It is the way back. It becomes visible as we give up our own pagan efforts to be right and allow God's grace to work in us in all things the will of our Father in heaven, a house that will never fall, no matter what.

Deuteronomy 11:18.26-28.32 / Romans 3:21-25.28 / Matthew 7:21-27

Twelfth Sunday

What I say to you in the dark, tell in the daylight; what you hear in whispers, proclaim from the housetops.

Jeremiah, brothers and sisters in Christ, is one of the four major prophets to whose names substantial writings are attached in the Old Testament. The other three are Isaiah, Ezekiel and Daniel. A prophet is someone chosen by God, usually under protest, to speak for God and act for God in a particular time and place. By definition the prophet is not well liked by his or her community. A prophet stirs things up. A prophet unsettles people. A false prophet easily gets caught out for telling people what they want to hear and attracting an unsuitable popularity. There is no quiet life for the genuine prophet. His only hope is that his God will look after him.

Every genuine prophet can make his own those words of today's psalm: It is for you that I suffer taunts, that shame covers my face, that I have become a stranger to my brothers, an alien to my own mother's sons. I burn with zeal for your house and taunts against you fall on me. The assurance that all will be well in the end, in the thick of it, with terror from every side, is diluted by the most devastating self-doubt. What if I am completely mistaken? What if I am completely deluded? What if I am completely mad?

The disciple of Jesus will know similar experiences, for every disciple of Jesus is in his or her own particular circumstances in a very personal way a prophet for Jesus, a witness to the truth about Jesus. To disciples who have reached a similar point in their discipleship, Jesus says simply: Do not be afraid. Do not be afraid that you might have got it wrong. Proclaim it from the house-tops. Do not be afraid of those who can kill the body but cannot kill the soul. Do not be afraid. Stick with me and I will stick with you. There is no need to afraid.

Fear is the death of the soul. Fear is the trapdoor of sin through which we plummet into hell. The message of

Jesus is that there is no need to be afraid. Yes we have all sinned, that is the way we are. But Jesus saves. His grace is freely available to all who accept him as their saviour. All who accept him as their saviour are enabled to begin a new life as children of God. There is absolutely no need to be afraid. This is the core message of Jesus. We must often wonder why we have created such a conspiracy of silence around something so important, something so exciting, something so decisive. What I say to you in the dark, says Jesus, tell in the daylight; what you hear in whispers, proclaim from the housetops.

But of course it takes courage even to whisper in the dark what we believe about Jesus, let alone telling it in the daylight and proclaiming it from the housetops. It takes courage to risk being a prophet for Jesus in this time and place that is so uniquely ours.

Jeremiah 20:10-13 / Romans 5:12-15 / Matthew 10:26-33

Thirteenth Sunday

You too must consider yourselves to be dead to sin but alive for God in Christ Jesus.

Dead to sin but alive for God, brothers and sisters in Christ. Dead to sin but alive for God. That sums up very well what we aspire to as Christians. Perhaps I could be so bold as to suggest that you might carry those two little phrases with you through this coming week and try to tease out more precisely what they might mean for you personally. Dead to sin but alive for God.

In the past, perhaps more so than today, many Christians, or so at least it is often said. were guilt-ridden in an unhealthy neurotic kind of obsession with sin. They were terrified of their God in an unpleasant twisted way that had nothing at all to do with that wonder and awe in God's presence our Confirmation children are nowadays taught is the beautiful substance of a genuine fear of the Lord in the biblical sense. The religious question has long since taken on a different shape. The loss of any sense of God has gone hand in hand with a loss of any sense of sin as all that comes between us and our God. If we find we no longer have any sense of sin it might well be that we no longer have much sense of God either and it might be as well to admit as much. There is no point to a God that we don't need.

There are many false gods. They do really exist in one way or another. Some of them are pleasant enough. The less pleasant ones entangle us in their superstitious devotions and make our lives a misery. They do really exist. It's just that they're not really gods at all. If we are to be dead to sin but alive to God we need to aspire to real faith in the true God. We need to know our need of God. We need to know that we are sinners who need to be saved.

Every year between Ash Wednesday and Pentecost Sunday we are offered an opportunity to re-live on a grand scale the whole process of our Baptism. Every year the Church provides us with a dramatic programme to advance our own personal Christening, which is of course the work of a lifetime. Every year Lent and Easter and Pentecost prod us to make yet another fresh start and die once and for all to sin and become alive for God in a definitive and conscious way. Saint Paul provides an excellent summary of the process in his letter to the Romans: When we were baptised in Christ Jesus we were baptised in his death. When we were baptised we went into the tomb with him and joined him in death so that we too might live a new life.

As Christians, as disciples of Jesus, we aspire to be really dead to sin and really alive for God. We do not fear the truth. We do not fear the truth about ourselves. We do not fear the truth about God. In fact we re-live the drama of our Baptism every time we make space in our days for prayer. We re-live the drama of our Baptism every time we take part in the Mass. We re-live the drama of our Baptism every time we struggle towards a right moral decision and actually doing the right thing.

We become worthy of Jesus as we take up our cross and follow in his footsteps.

Second Kings 4:8-11.14-16 / Romans 6:3-4.8-11 / Matthew 10:37-42

Fourteenth Sunday

Come to me, all you who labour and are overburdened, and I will give you rest.

It is impossible for us to hear these words without emotion, brothers and sisters in Christ, because we know that they are addressed directly to us. Come to me, all you who labour and are overburdened, and I will give you rest. Shoulder my yoke and learn from me, for I am gentle and humble in heart, and you will find rest for your souls. But have we really heard these words, addressed to us in the darkest moments of our lives? Perhaps not. For God has indeed hidden these things from the learned and the clever and revealed them only to those who approach him with the naive confidence of children.

The naive confidence of children - something the learned and the clever have lost somewhere along the way. Of course we need to emerge from childhood, to establish our independence and forge our own way of seeing things. In this process of growing up we all acquire certain valuable competences - but whence this arrogance that we know everything about everything, that there is nothing new to learn, even about life itself? The learned have worked it all out, they know exactly what God requires of them. And the clever know, with breathe-taking precision, how much they can get away with. Yet at a certain point the shallowness of their lives is revealed in an anxious striving. Jesus has pity on them for they labour and are over-burdened more than most. He proposes an alternative to their anxious striving: Shoulder my yoke and learn from me, for I am gentle and humble of heart, and you will find rest for your souls. This is the way back to the naive confidence of the child as our anxious striving becomes a gracious cooperation with the inevitable, the will of God for us. Yes, my yoke is easy, says Jesus, and my burden light.

But how are the learned and the clever to become gentle and humble in heart? Is there any hope for them at all? Saint Paul knows the secret of

it - from his own personal experience. Your interests, he reminds us,
are not in the unspiritual, but in the
spiritual, since the Spirit of God has
made his home in you. The trap for
the learned and the clever is that
there is an unspiritual way of being
interested in spiritual things. They
see the advantages of religion. They
suspect there might be some- thing in
it for them. It looks somehow like a
superior recipe for success, a better
way of getting what they want. But
God is not mocked. God cannot be
used. Whatever we imagine him to
be, he is something else. God is not
the answer to any of our questions.
God is not the solution to any of our
problems. God is the answer to a
question we had never asked, the
solution to a problem we didn't
know we had.

Once we allow the Spirit of God to
make his home in us there is no
further necessity, in Saint Paul's
words, for us to obey our unspiritual
selves or to live unspiritual lives. The
learned and the clever cannot see that
from where they stand. The gentle
and humble in heart, with all the

naive confidence of children, have allowed Jesus to take them by the hand and lead them over and beyond to his own vantage point from where alone we can enjoy the spiritual panorama of all things seen though the eyes of God and so enter fully into the glorious freedom of his children, an easy yoke and a light burden indeed.

Zechariah 9:9-10 / Romans 8:9.11-13 / Matthew 11:25-30

Fifteenth Sunday

The heart of this nation has grown coarse, their ears are dull of hearing, and they have shut their eyes, for they fear that they should see with their eyes, hear with their ears, understand with their heart, and be converted and be healed by me.

These sad words, brothers and sisters in Christ, were addressed from God through the Prophet Isaiah to the chosen people some two thousand seven hundred years ago. Jesus thought it appropriate to repeat them in his day. And here and now they jump out of the gospel at us with a certain unwelcome freshness. For they have lost none of their relevance. They are just as relevant in this time and place that is uniquely ours as ever they were. But Jesus has made them Gospel words and Gospel words, even such dark and terrible words, are good news when we allow them to show us the truth about ourselves, when we allow them to light up those dark and terrible places of our hearts that we would rather not be reminded about. There is pain in that but it is a pain that leads to conversion and healing.

The parable of the sower comes to each one of us in the here and now of our own personal situation. They are words of healing but first we must face the pain. What sort of welcome have we for this word of God just now? What sort of soil is the seed sown in when it is sown in us today?

As he sowed some seeds fell on the edge of the path and the birds came and ate them up. Those who hear without understanding: we are not talking here about an intellectual grasp of abstract principles. For it is with the heart that the message is heard and understood or not at all.

Other seeds fell on patches of rock where they sprang up straightaway but as soon as the sun came up they were scorched and they withered away. Yes, sometimes the beauty of the Christian way fills us with joy and comfort but actually putting it into practice quickly proves to be altogether too inconvenient.

Other seeds fell among thorns and the thorns grew up and choked them. Yes, the one thing necessary that the Gospel sets before us pales into insignificance as we struggle with the entanglements of wealth and pleasure and our paralysing anxieties about status and success.

Other seeds fell on rich soil and produced their crop, some a hundredfold, some sixty, some thirty. This is the message of hope in today's Gospel: when we have served our apprenticeship of discourage-ment and despair on the edge of the path, on the patches of rock and fallen among thorns, God in his kindness will take the brokenness of our lives and heal us with his life and his love. This is surely what Saint Paul means when he shares with us his thought that what we suffer in this life can never be compared to the glory, as yet unrevealed, which is waiting for us when at last we have really heard and understood what God is saying to us through Jesus, sometimes dramatically but mostly in the ordinary circumstances of our daily lives.

Happy are your eyes because they see and your ears because they hear: Many holy people longed to see what you see and never saw it. Many holy people longed to hear what you hear and never heard it.

Isaiah 55:10-11 / Romans 8:18-23 / Matthew 13:1-23

Sixteenth Sunday

I will speak to you in parables and expound things hidden since the foundation of the world.

One of our great mistakes, brothers and sisters in Christ, is that we try too hard. We rake over our past, torturing ourselves with guilt about how different the present could be if only we had done this or that. And we exert ourselves to control as much as possible the future evolution of our circumstances. By trying too hard we miss the presence of God in our lives.

The parables we have heard in today's gospel are an invitation to serenity. To put our trust in God is to plant, humbly and quietly, the little seed that we have been given and then watch it grow without any anxious interference. Humbly and quietly we mix our seemingly insignificant quantity of yeast with the flour and leave it to do its own work in its own time. Above all, we are not to excite ourselves about the way the world is. God can be counted upon to sort all that out in the end.

It is pointless to try to change the world if we do not first allow God to change us. Until we tune into God and allow him to refashion us in accordance with his will we have no right to change anyone or anything. We cannot change anyone or anything for the better when all we are doing is seeking our own convenience, acting out our pride, bullying others to conform to our prejudices, trying vainly to make ourselves feel better.

We need to learn patience - with others and with ourselves. The patience of God surprises us. It will be time enough to separate the good wheat from the bad weeds at the end. In the meantime, here and now, we need to learn to live in the world as it is, we need to learn to live in the Church as it is, we need to learn to live with the people we have been given to live with. We need to learn to live with ourselves, to accept our past, to receive our present as the gift that it is and to entrust our future into the hands of a God about whom we know only that he loves us.

Many of you will already know that little serenity prayer which puts this concisely and splendidly. Lord, grant me the patience to accept what I cannot change, the courage to change what I need to change and the wisdom to know the difference. We cannot live as we ought in this, world without prayer of this kind. The Spirit comes to help us in our weakness, as Saint Paul assures us. When we cannot choose words in order to pray properly, the Spirit himself expresses our plea in a way that could never be put into words. This is true prayer, God in the very depths of our being crying out to God beyond all the limitations of our world. When our lives are transfigured by such prayer we receive as much patience, courage and wisdom as we need, our hearts are at peace and our world becomes a marginally better place.

Wisdom 12:13.16-19 / Romans 8:26-27 / Matthew 13:24-43

Seventeenth Sunday

We know that by turning everything to their good God cooperates with all those who love him.

Wisdom, brothers and sisters in Christ, is an attractive quality but, as we quickly learn, it can be neither bought with money nor achieved by effort. It is a gift that comes directly from God. If we are to be ready to receive so precious a gift a first step we might need to take would be to make a list of all those things that make us unhappy and begin to consider how we might best go about giving them up.

Wisdom is the unsuspected treasure hidden in the field of our bitterest experiences. We are ploughing away, striving for something that matters desperately to us, when suddenly we stumble across it, this hidden treasure - and we know at once that it makes sense to let go of everything else and make that treasure our own. Wisdom is that pearl of great price worth infinitely more than all the rest put together.

We feel the joy of the man who found the treasure in the field. It was the last thing he was expecting and yet at once he knew what he needed to do. We sense too the joy of the merchant. He had been looking and had already known a certain success but nothing had prepared him for the sight of this one pearl and the chance to make it his own. What would it be like for us to see so great a joy within our grasp? What would it be like for us to be overwhelmed at last by wisdom and enlightenment?

Let us start making that list of the things that make us unhappy. Perhaps we have been striving for something foolish, waiting for something that will never happen, failing to move on even though we know the time has come. There are so many recipes for unhappiness. We want material things, we are driven by ambitions for ourselves or for our families, we need the affection of this or that person: so many splendid recipes for pain and disappointment. Wisdom, we sense, would involve setting out in a different direction, having the courage to abandon the familiar and strike out into the unknown.

Perhaps we are like that man in the field – not looking for wisdom at all. Or perhaps we are like that merchant - committed in principle to the pearl of great price but somehow just too easily content with the cheap, the vulgar and the false. The young Solomon shows us a better way. His example invites us to turn humbly to God in our hearts, ask for his gift of wisdom and ready ourselves to receive it. A pleasant alternative, one might think, to the eternal weeping - and grinding of teeth.

First Kings 3:5.7-12 / Romans 8:28-30 / Matthew 13:44-52

Eighteenth Sunday

There is no need for them to go: give them something to eat yourselves. But they answered, All we have with us is five loaves and two fish.

Part of the moral message of our religion, brothers and sisters in Christ, is undoubtedly that, we should count our blessings and know that however disadvantaged we might think ourselves in all kinds of ways we have in fact more than we really need and that sharing what we do not need with those less fortunate than ourselves is not so much a matter of charity as of justice.

The message of today's Gospel is, however, something entirely different. It is about the miracle that happens when, aware of our poverty, we nevertheless take the risk of sharing all that we have and are.

We are told that when he humbled himself to share in our humanity Jesus emptied himself and entered into our poverty. There can have been few moments in his life before the agony in the garden when he felt that poverty more intensely than at this moment when he received the news that John the Baptist had been executed by Herod. He seeks to be alone but the thankless and ungracious crowd pursues him. He knows that, in the end, he too will be their victim but somehow he can do no other than take pity on them. It is the compassionate awareness that those who cause the most suffering to others are often those who themselves have been made to suffer more than most. Jesus does not preach at them. His pity expresses itself on this occasion in the healing way he spends the day with them.

Evening comes and the disciples ask him to send the crowd away. It is the reasonable and responsible thing to do. The disciples can't feed them so they should be sent off to fend for themselves. No doubt we do the same thing all the time ourselves. It is the easy way out and Jesus refuses to take it. On a day when he had so much wanted to be alone he had experienced for himself that there can be no running away from the

54

suffering of others. He was well aware that there were only five loaves and two fish but his insight is that our own poverty is never an excuse for ignoring the needs of others: There is no need for them to go - give them something to eat yourselves. It is an insight large enough to provoke a miracle.

We can just imagine the horror of the disciples when Jesus asks for their five loaves and two fish. Then he raised his eyes to heaven and said the blessing. And breaking the loaves he handed them to his disciples who gave them to the crowds. And horror melts into an unexpected lightness of heart: they all ate as much as they wanted, and they collected the scraps remaining, twelve baskets full. It is the miracle of the Mass itself: we are invited to risk the offering of all we have and are and in the blessing and breaking of the bread Jesus melts and moulds our selfish horror into a lightness of heart that brings life to the world, the certainty, as Saint Paul puts it, that nothing can ever come between us and the love of God

made visible in Christ Jesus our
Lord.

*Isaiah 55:1-3 / Romans 8:35.37-39 /
Matthew 14:13-21*

Nineteenth Sunday

As soon as he felt the force of the wind, he took fright and began to sink.

An experience familiar to us all, brothers and sisters in Christ. We have the best of intentions but the shock of real action unnerves us and we flounder. We are people of little faith. Our personal drama is lived out between faith and fear, between courage and doubt.

Faith is about trusting life because we trust God our Father who created us. Faith is about trusting ourselves because we trust the Lord Jesus Christ who redeemed us by his death on the cross. Faith is about trusting one another because we trust the Spirit of God filling our hearts and gathering us together into the Church.

Faith is the answer to fear. But fear returns to haunt us and undermines our faith. Fear cuts us off from God our Father and leaves us terrified of life. Fear distances us from the Lord

Jesus Christ. It abandons us to our sinfulness and leaves us afraid of ourselves, anxious about what will become of us. Fear drives out the Spirit of God from our hearts leaving us afraid of one another and excluding us from the fellowship of those who believe.

There are, of course, lives of sheer terror untouched by faith - and there are those whose faith has taken them beyond fear once and for all. But for the rest of us, people of little faith that we are, our drama is lived out between faith and fear, between courage and doubt. Like the disciples in today's Gospel we do indeed believe. But our littleness of faith is shown up in times of crisis when fear betrays us into panic and we sink.

We are born into fear - that is the essence of original sin. But Jesus comes to set us free. Strangely his coming is not immediately reassureing. Like the disciples in the storm-tossed boat we see him coming towards us out of the night and we are terrified even as he calls out to us: Courage! It is I! Do not be afraid.

What are we afraid of at such a moment? Freedom has its own special terrors. It suddenly occurs to us that we are, after all, alright as we are, thank you very much. Yes, we would rather freedom passed us by. Lord, if it is you, tell me to come to you across the water - this is Peter's prayer of faith. Come, Jesus invites him. But Peter is a man of little faith and as soon as he feels the force of the wind he takes fright and begins to sink. Lord, save me! he cries. It is his prayer of fear.

We too have our prayers of faith, and our prayers of fear. It is not by strength of character or severe determination of will that we can overcome the weakness of our faith and the pervasive energy of our fear. Rather it is by prayer that faith is strengthened and fear faced. It is natural to pray when we are afraid. It is not even necessary to believe in God to pray at such times. Somehow it just comes naturally.

The daily discipline of prayer that grounds our trust in life and allows us to walk across the waters of every fear does not have at all the same natural spontaneity. Jesus sent the crowds away and went up into the hills by himself to pray. That was the secret of his strength. People of little faith like us need to find their own quiet place where they can tune into the quietness of God. To a world in panic this daily discipline of prayer is a provocative waste of time and yet it is the very thing, the only thing, that allows God to transform our anxious strivings into a gracious service of one another in generosity and love.

First Kings 19:9.11-13 / Romans 9:1-5 / Matthew 14:22-33

Twentieth Sunday

Lord, she said, help me.

Our prayers are always answered,
brothers and sisters in Christ.
Today's gospel is a lesson in how it
happens. This gentile woman has
heard that Jesus works miracles. Out
she comes and starts shouting, Sir,
Son of David, take pity on me. My
daughter is tormented by a devil.
Somehow we can all come to terms
with what happens to ourselves in
life. We might almost think it an
unworthy prayer to ask God to help
us in our own personal difficulties.
What is truly unbearable is to have to
watch helplessly the torment of
someone we love, someone whom
life has entrusted to our care. Sir,
Son of David, take pity on me. My
daughter is tormented by a devil. It is
a mother's prayer, a mother so de-
mented by grief that she cannot even
think what miracle to ask for. But
Jesus answered her not a word. Often
our own prayers are answered in
precisely this way, by the silence of
God. And silence is an answer - as
we all know from letters and e-mails

that remain unacknowledged and telephone calls that are not returned.

His disciples plead with him. Give her what she wants, they said, because she is shouting after us. This is a prayer too, though a particularly trivial form of prayer. We are all capable of it. Storming heaven I think some call it. It misunderstands miracles and misses the point about prayer. Miracles are not magic, they happen of themselves when the spark of faith transforms a person's heart. Jesus is not a magician. His divine gift is that he understands the human heart and knows how to lead us to the insight that we need. Our silliness is to think that prayer is about changing God and getting things our own way. When we really pray it is we who are changed and allowed to see things God's way.

What does Jesus do for this desperate woman? What insight does she need for her daughter to be well again? There is no mention of a husband. We sense that she must carry the whole burden of her daughter alone. Perhaps that is the problem. Children that are more smothered than mothered are condemned to a tormented existence. Not the least tragedy of such possessive love is that by caring too much for others we deprive them of their own responsibility for themselves and of their will to live their own lives. Any wonder they torment themselves and us.

Jesus is not a magician and he does not apologize for it. I was sent only to the lost sheep of the House of Israel, he tells his disciples. He recognizes a limit to his responsibility. But the woman has come up to him and is kneeling at his feet. She renews her prayer. Lord, she says, help me. It is the moment of truth. It is not fair to take the children's food and throw it to the house-dogs. It sounds harsh and even rude but it does the trick. The woman realizes that just as there is a limit to what Jesus can be responsible for so too there is a limit to her responsibility for her daughter. She does not need anything more than the scraps from the master's table. She now knows that she has been asking too much of God and of life, of herself and of her daughter. Woman, you have great faith, Jesus commends her – emphasising the source of the miracle. Let your wish be granted. And so it is that she goes home to find a very different daughter waiting for her very different mother.

When we persevere in prayer we become nicer people and that solves any number of problems.

Isaiah 56:1.6-7 / Romans 11:13-15.29-32 / Matthew 15:21-28

Twenty-First Sunday

But you, he said, who do you say I am?

The question of who Jesus is, brothers and sisters in Christ, is not a question that can be answered once and for all. It is, rather, a question that accompanies us on our journey through life. We catch glimpses. We garner fragments. But we never have the full picture. You are the Christ, the Son of the living God, said Peter. He spoke for us all. They are the right words. But what do they mean?

Peter's profession of faith is the rock upon which Jesus builds his Church. The Church is the great gathering together of all who share this faith and by their faith belong to Christ and bear the name of Christian. But faith is a personal matter. We believe together, but we cannot believe for one another. And so it is that the words of Jesus reach out to us from today's gospel and challenge us directly and personally: You, he says, who do you say I am?

It is somehow an awkward question. But then do we ever really know another person? Do we ever really know ourselves? Who are you? Who am I? - these are the basic questions that reveal the meaning of our lives. From the moment we are born to the moment we die we are constantly being told who we are. We need to silence all that: chatter and gossip, prejudice and stereotyping, conditioning and tradition - there is no escape. We are constantly being told who we are. Not least by people who say they love us: they desperately need us to know who we have to be to keep them happy and that, of course is manipulation and not love at all. Love dares to ask us quietly and gently who we are - in such a way that the question can begin at last to be really answered.

Until we find our way to the place where this question of who we are can be addressed we will understand little or nothing either about Jesus or about life. The question of who we are and the question of who he is are strangely intertwined.

You are the Christ, the Son of the living God, said Peter. It is not the sort of information that can be passed around - by gossips or by the media or even by intellectuals. It was not flesh and blood that revealed this to you, Peter, but the Father in heaven. It is the solid rock of faith upon which the Church can be built, a place of community and freedom where there is a mutual binding and loosing that is the flourishing of love both human and divine.

We hear about Jesus all our lives. At home - perhaps, at school - certainly, in Church - sometimes. We might read a book about him. There are films too and television programmes. There are above all the Gospels and the other writings of the New Testament. But until we learn to sit quietly in his presence - before the crucifix or his icon or the tabernacle, in the Church or indeed, as he himself suggested, in the silence and privacy of our room - we will never really know him at all. What are we to say to him? There is a simple prayer that has always led his disciples into the fullness of truth: Lord Jesus Christ,

Son of the living God, be merciful to me a sinner.

Isaiah 22:19-23 / Romans 11:33-36 / Matthew 16:13-20

Twenty-Second Sunday

Get behind me, Satan! You are an obstacle in my path, because the way you think is not God's way but man's.

An abrupt change of tone, brothers and sisters in Christ! For to the same man we heard Jesus say in last Sunday's gospel: You are Peter, and on this rock I will build my Church. Peter recognized in Jesus the long awaited Messiah but he did not as yet understand that the whole meaning of who Jesus is was to be revealed in his suffering and death on the cross. He reacts to Jesus' intimation of what was to come as we would no doubt react ourselves: Heaven preserve you, Lord. This must not happen to you.

Peter did not then realise that the foolishness of God is wiser than any human wisdom and he takes Jesus aside and remonstrates with him. And in this he finds a following down through the centuries in the religious sentimentality and comforting chatter of those who revolt at the hard word of the Cross. Their way of thinking is not God's way but man's. And we must be resolute in evading their trap because everything is at stake: Get behind me, Satan! You are an obstacle in my path.

It was, you remember, a temptation Jesus had already faced and conquered, Satan's last desperate attempt to divert him from his course. He took him then to a very high mountain and showed him all the kingdoms of the world and he said to him: All these I will give you if you will fall down and worship me. And Jesus had sent him on his way once and for all: Be gone, Satan, for it is written: You shall worship the Lord your God and him only shall you serve.

Peter naively serves up this old temptation again and there is a moment of black humour as the rock upon which the Church is to be built becomes an obstacle in the Saviour's path. Peter, for all his fine words and pleasing sentiments, is still thinking the thoughts of men rather than of God. His human thought patterns have not yet been blown away by the mystery of the cross. His heart is still set on some kind of worldly success rather than the fulfilment of the mysterious purposes of God.

There is something of this in all of us. We are always caught somewhere between faith and doubt as we make our own way of the cross, summoned by the promise of entering into the glory of God. We sense that there are no short cuts, but we are tempted at every turn.

It helps us to know that Jesus faced this same temptation and we need to hear the words of radically challenging encouragement that he speaks to us at the crucial moments of our lives: If anyone wants to be a follower of mine, let them renounce themself and take up their cross and follow me.

This law of the cross is the law of life. A truly fulfilled life eludes the grasp of those who selfishly seek self-fulfilment. Only those who cease to grasp at life, only those who abandon their petty projects for a made-to-measure passage through this world, only those who surrender themselves to God in imitation of Jesus, only they will enter into the fullness of life. The alternative is really too terrible to contemplate.

What will we have gained if we get everything we want, win the whole world, only in exchange for the ruination of our own life, the loss of our soul?

Jeremiah 20:7-9 / Romans 12:1-2 / Matthew 16:21-27

Twenty-Third Sunday

You must love your neighbour as yourself. Love is the one thing that cannot hurt your neighbour. That is why it is the answer to every one of the commandments.

Today's Scripture readings, brothers and sisters in Christ, speak to us of the responsibility we have for one another. Am I my brother's keeper? That is a question that has echoed insolently down through human history, expressing a selfish refusal of responsibility - the insolent question of a murderer refusing to acknowledge his crime. For murder is the ultimate expression of refusal of responsibility for another person.

We are in fact responsible for one another in a whole variety of ways. Christians have learnt from Jesus to understand this responsibility in terms of love and in terms of community. It is a richer kind of love, a richer form of community than anything we are used to in our experience of the world. Jesus offers us a different kind of community, beyond selfishness, where he promises to be with us himself enabling us to love in that special, selfless, life-giving way that he loves us.

We are responsible, in love and in community, for our neighbour. And who is my neighbour? Yes, that is another question that can be used insolently to justify the exclusion of others from the scope of our concern, whether people in need at the other side of the globe or people suffering alone around the corner. The message of Jesus is uncompromising on this responsibility we have for one another. He died for us all - without exception. And he gave us the parable of the Good Samaritan lest we should ever fail to recognize him in another's need. For, yes, my neighbour is always that person or group of people who in this very moment have most urgent need of me and whatever I can do for them.

Am I my brother's keeper? Who is my neighbour? We can continue to ask these questions defensively and use them to deny responsibility for others. We can go on living splendidly for ourselves alone. Or we can face up to responsibilities we have been avoiding and decide to do something positive. Let us take a few moments to seize today the grace Jesus has won for us and make that decision now. Love, Saint Paul reminds us, is the one thing that cannot hurt our neighbour. That is why it is the answer to every one of the commandments.

Ezekiel 33:7-9 / Romans 13:8-10 / Matthew 18:15-20

Twenty-Fourth Sunday

Resentment and anger, these are foul things, and both are found with the sinner.

The first thing to be said about forgiveness, brothers and sisters in Christ, is that it is of immense advantage to the person who forgives. Your enemies grow fat on the grudge you bear them. When we let go of our grudges enemies are disarmed. In fact in this matter of forgiveness we are our own worst enemies where we could be our own best friends.

Resentment and anger, these are foul things, and both are found with the sinner. Indeed they are the clearest symptoms of sin. Forgive your neighbour the hurt he does you, and when you pray, you sins will be forgiven. This priceless wisdom from the Jewish scriptures Jesus has set as the chief jewel in the prayer-text he taught his disciples: Forgive us our trespasses as we forgive those who trespass against us.

Father, forgive us our trespasses as we forgive those who trespass against us. St Augustine calls this prayer our daily baptism. Every time we say it the life of grace is renewed within us and all our sins are washed away. At least that is what happens when our hearts are in harmony with our words. Otherwise it is an awesome bargain with God that is not perhaps entirely to our advent-age: Forgive us our trespasses as we forgive those who trespass against us. If God were to forgive us in exactly the same measure as we forgive others there are certainly times when it wouldn't add up to much.

Look again at that first reading, the wise words of Ecclesiasticus: If a man nurses anger against another, can he then demand compassion from the Lord? Showing no pity for a man like himself, can he then plead for his own sins? Mere creature of flesh, he cherishes resentment; who will forgive him his sins? What a predicament this puts us in. Our enemies grow fat on the grudge we bear them while we are eaten away by resentment and anger, these foul things that are found in every sinner.

Ecclesiasticus has a suggestion: Remember the last things, and stop hating, remember dissolution and death. Shall we try it right now? Imagine a coffin here before the altar, the way there is at a funeral. See yourself coming up to have a look at the name on it. It is your name. And what is left of you in this world, your remains in a word, are reverently enclosed within it. Allow yourself to feel what that is like. Feel the peace, the cool. No more hatred. No more anger. No more resentment.

Lord, how often must I forgive my brother if he wrongs me? I think we know the answer well enough.

Ecclesiasticus 27:30 – 28:7 / Romans 14:7-9 / Matthew 18:21-35

Twenty-Fifth Sunday

My thoughts are not your thoughts, my ways not your ways - it is the Lord who speaks.

The danger is, brothers and sisters in Christ, that we, each of us, create our God in our own image and likeness. It is a recipe for disappointment and bewilderment. And when it comes to the crunch the message of the living God to each one of us is perfectly clear: Yes, the heavens are as high above earth as my ways are above your ways, my thoughts above your thoughts.

Thus, for example, the last will be first, and the first, last. What could be more unjust in human terms? What could be more distressing to the hardened believer with strong views about how God ought to behave? I have even seen people fighting over the lowest place so as to be sure of getting where they want to be in the end. But getting where exactly? What if the first will always be last? God is not mocked. God is beyond the reach of all the manipu--

lations we practise upon one another. We are the chief victims of our own deceptions.

Why have you been standing here idle all day? An interesting and provocative question that - if we hear it addressed to us today from a God whose thoughts are not our thoughts, his ways not our ways. Why have you been standing here idle all day, the whole day of your life up to this present moment? Yes, it is an interesting and provocative question. We might react angrily and want to let God know that we are, and always have been, extremely busy with never a moment to ourselves. Or we might react with bitterness and explode in the face of God with all our well rehearsed excuses for the emptiness of our lives. But actually it is a friendly enough question, addressed to us in the perplexity of our daily experience by a God who loves us and somehow strangely needs us. We might react initially with anger or bitterness but to really hear this question coming to us from God is to find something stir deep within us filling us with consolation and renewing our hope. Our past is of no account, no matter what great store we might set by it, or however much it weighs us down. It is this present moment carrying us into the future that counts: For God is offering us employment, our own little place in his great plan. And he will pay us our denarius, the day's wages of the unskilled labourer in the ancient world - not much in truth, no security for tomorrow certainly, but enough for today, all that we really need, the answer to our modest prayer for our daily bread, the fulfilment of God's purpose in our lives here and now in the present moment, preparing us for the glory that is to come.

Seek the Lord while he is still to be found, call to him while he is still near.

Avoid anything in your everyday lives that would be unworthy of the Gospel of Christ.

Isaiah 55:6-9 / Philippians 1:20-24.27 / Matthew 20:1-16

Twenty-Sixth Sunday

Always consider the other person to be better than yourself.

It is not easy, brothers and sisters in Christ, consistently to consider the other person to be better than ourself. We might humbly make exception for the great and the good but our tendency is to judge those we encounter in our more immediate environment. Our tendency is to judge those closest to us and do them down – whether in the wild delight of gossip or the smugness of self-congratulation or the subtle insinuations of faint praise. History can judge the people of the past because the past is forever fixed and unalterable but a living human being cannot be judged because he or she is not yet what they will be. We are not today what we may still become and so it is that we may hope, in the end, whatever our past, to be one with God in this life and for the life to come. The wise thing is to call no one happy, or indeed unhappy, until they be dead, until death has intervened to seal their fate forever.

Consider the two sons in today's parable. The one says yes to his father but does not go. The other boy says no but afterwards thinks better of it and goes. Most of us, I suppose, have said a sort of yes to God. That is why we are at Mass today. But it is hard to stomach the idea that greater sinners than us - Jesus mentions specifically those unpleasant tax collectors and the painted prostitutes of his day - are making their way into the kingdom before us. The parable does not tell us that the father actually knew or even cared which of his sons had done the work. No doubt the yes-man was happy to take the credit for it.

There are those among us who consider appearance more important than reality. There are those who attach more importance to what people think about them than the truth about themselves. Some conform out of indifference and others out of self-interest. And then on the other side there are those who rebel and yet somehow in their very rebellion find the grace to do what

God really wants. The sinner receives the grace of forgiveness and life while the self-righteous fall away, for they know no need of grace. In a surprising sense the sinner is free to accept God's invitation. The self-righteous are prisoners of their own conceited idea that they have it all worked out, even God and his kingdom. If unpleasant tax collectors and painted prostitutes are making their way into anything before them, then clearly that is not something for them.

In this life each one of us moves at his or her own pace - in the things of God as much as in anything else. There is growth and there is decay. There is an inching forward and a slipping back. God's invitation is to begin afresh every day, every moment - whatever the past has been. It is an invitation that rarely comes in a dramatic way. It arises gently but persistently out of the circumstances of our lives and the needs of those who are our nearest neighbours. Always consider the other person to be better than yourself so that nobody thinks of his own interests first but everybody thinks of other people's interests instead. In your minds you must be the same as Christ Jesus.

Ezekiel 18:25-28 / Philippians 2:1-11 / Matthew 21:28-32

Twenty-Seventh Sunday

My friend had a vineyard on a fertile hillside.... He expected it to yield grapes, but sour grapes were all that it gave.

There are passages in Scripture that are so sad, brothers and sisters in Christ, that we would rather not attend to them and yet they ring so true that we cannot but be touched by them. These passages about God's vineyard are of this kind - so truly sad and so sadly true.

Let me sing to my friend the song of his love for his vineyard. The vineyard is God's. He has entrusted it to us in love and as happens in the vulnerability of love he has left himself and his vineyard entirely at our mercy. We forget all this and treat the vineyard as if it were our own. We forget that we have nothing that we have not received from the hand of God. We become arrogant and ungracious. We adopt a strategy of selfishness that is not ultimately in our own best interest. The kingdom of God will be taken from you and

given to a people who will produce
its fruit. Sour grapes all round.

The vineyard is our life. Our time
and place in the great scheme of
things. Our little life, fenced around
with all our little limitations. Our
limitations that we so often fight
against - not recognizing in them our
cross and our treasure. Until wisdom
comes we fail to see that the
acceptance of our limitations is our
richest source of possibilities for
growth and happiness and fulfilment.
We are to carry our cross and
uncover our treasure for all the world
to see.

Into the vineyard of our life God
sends his servants to enquire about
the fruits of our existence, the love,
the joy and the peace that are the
fruits of his Spirit in us. These
messengers that God sends to us -
people who have touched our lives in
unexpected ways, experiences that
have warmed our souls, the awaken-
ing of our inner longings for truth
and goodness and beauty - how have
we treated these messengers of God?
Have we not too often silenced them,

and killed them, by our striving in our blindness and our selfishness to make our own what belongs for ever and always to God, - our life and its fruits.

Finally he sent his son to them. They will respect my son, he said. Do we fully realise that Jesus is our last chance? Will we kill him too? Or will we allow him to take charge of our vineyard and make it his own? When the tenants saw the son they said to each other: This is the heir. Come on, let us kill him and take over his inheritance. There is a gruesome inevitability about the killing of Jesus. There is a real part of each one of us that feels threatened by goodness in others. We regret too late the anger and violence it evokes in us. And yet our regret may somehow blossom into repentance and give birth to hope. We have killed goodness as surely as if we had stood with the crowd on Good Friday crying out for his crucifixion. But in the goodness of that Friday there is the promise of Easter, the promise of resurrection, the promise of new life. The stone rejected by the builders has become the cornerstone. This was the Lord's doing and it is wonderful to see.

Is it really so difficult, when all is said and done, to surrender to God what belongs to God and sit back and enjoy the spectacle of his grace unfolding in our lives?

Isaiah 5:1-7 / Philippians 4:6-9 / Matthew 21:33-43

Twenty-Eighth Sunday

*How did you get in here, my friend,
without a wedding garment?*

A dramatic reminder, brothers and sisters in Christ, that though we may well have found ourselves herded into the Church with the rest of the crowd, it is our own responsibility to ensure that we satisfy the entry requirements. A Baptism certificate is not enough.

A moment of truth will come when we will be called upon to speak for ourselves. And there will be no refuge in silence. Many are called but few are chosen. This is the paradox of the Church in the turmoil of history. The Church is open to everyone, no one is excluded from coming in and having a look round. The servants in the parable went out on to the roads and collected together everyone they could find, bad and good alike and the wedding hall was filled with guests. But at the same time there can be no hiding in the crowd: it is a matter for personal decision, an intensely personal decision. A personal decision made once and for all at the turning-point of our lives and renewed everyday in commitment and perseverance.

How did you get in here, my friend, without a wedding garment? The man was silent. It is the silence not of supplication but of insolence and indifference. And it has its own consequences. Many are called, but few are chosen: a hard saying perhaps. The place where God's generosity collides with our rebellion. Salvation is available to all, yes, but not all avail of it. It can no doubt be a great blessing to be born into a Christian environment and to be brought up in the Christian way but there are no second-hand wedding garments. And what is this wedding garment precisely, the want of which reveals our insolence and indifference? It is not some showy or extravagant attire. Nor is it some kind of uniform that makes us all the same. It is the simple, decent elegance of personal decision and personal commitment. It cannot be bought at any price but it is given, tailor-made, to each one who asks for it in prayer - prayer which says, and says again: Lord, I believe; help thou my unbelief.

Let that be our prayer today as we accept the king's invitation to his son's wedding feast. And as we welcome Jesus into our lives let us allow him to welcome us more fully into his Church. That is the sense of our Amen. Yes, the body of Christ: that is who we are, that is who we want to be. Today and every day. Now and forever.

Isaiah 25:6-10 / Philippians 4:12-14.19-20 / Matthew 22:1-14

Twenty-Ninth Sunday

O sing a new song to the Lord, sing to the Lord all the earth.

It is always time for a change, brothers and sisters in Christ, and it is never too late. Sing a new song to the Lord. This pressing invitation is always there, lying somewhere neglected in our lives, hidden under a pile of all kinds of other things we mean sometime to attend to. Sing a new song to the Lord, sing to the Lord all the earth.

We are to know the importance of God and act on it. I am the Lord, unrivalled, he reminds those he addresses through his prophet Isaiah. There is no other God besides me. From the rising to the setting of the sun, apart from, me, all is nothing. Yes, we are invited to know the importance of God and build our lives on it. But all the false gods of human experience are alive and well and, however unwittingly, we allow them to dominate our lives and blot out our remembrance of the one true

God who created us and calls us to himself.

All the false gods of human experience are alive and well and they dominate our lives. In the materialistic environment in which we live and move and have our being we think ourselves clever enough not to believe in such divinities and, of course, yes, they are indeed false gods, without substance. And yet they haunt our dreams, keep us awake at night and occupy us all day long for years on end until we catch ourselves on. In our world they have lost the old poetic names they had in ancient times but we can still identify their shrines and we know their names in plain English. Big among them are Sex and Money and Power and the pursuit of them banishes the one true God fro~ our lives. And they are unfaithful gods, for however blind our obedience, in the end they abandon us to stress and anxiety, disease and death.

Jesus gave a clever answer that day when they tried to trap him, the Pharisees who didn't think it right to pay taxes to a foreign government and Herod's supporters who thought it politically expedient to keep the Romans happy. Is it permissible to pay taxes to Caesar or not? Let me see the money you pay the tax with, says he. Ah yes, you all pay your taxes, you all carry the coinage on your person - it would seem that, in practice, you have already answered your own question.

Whose head is this? Whose name? Caesar's, they replied. Very well, give back to Caesar what belongs to Caesar, says Jesus - and he might have added by way of further explanation: Yes, I know the Romans worship him as a god but it really is perfectly alright to use his coinage and even to be grateful to him for running the economy. It's not a big deal that his name and image are stamped on your coins. The important thing is to remember God whose name and image are imprinted on your very soul. See that you give back to God what belongs to God.

Give back to God what belongs to God. It is time for a change. Sing a new song to the Lord. Begin at last, to respect his name and image hidden at the very core of your being and waiting to be revealed in the life of every man and woman you meet. Integrate your false gods into your lives and give them their proper place. Sex belongs in the chaste embrace of husband and wife. Money is essential for running the systems that support our lives. And when we find the power to take control of ourselves in freedom we no longer hunger for power over others. In everything, give back to God what belongs to God - his image in you and in those you love. Amen.

Isaiah 45:1.4-6 / First Thessalonians 1:1-5 / Matthew 22:15-21

Thirtieth Sunday

You must love the Lord your God with all your heart, with all your soul, and with all your mind. This is the greatest and the first commandment. The second resembles it: you must love your neighbour as yourself.

We are to love God, brothers and sisters in Christ. And we are to love our neighbour as we love ourself. The whole art of religion lies in living the right balance of these three loves: love of God, love of neighbour, love of self.

Caricatures are instructive. Some are so busy loving God that they have no time for anyone else, not even themselves. That can't be right. It cannot be the kind of religion that God wants. Others are so busy loving their neighbour that they never give a thought to themselves or indeed to God. That can't be right either. Commitment to others too often masks the fact that there is nothing behind our own façade. Others still are totally absorbed in loving themselves.

Jesus establishes priorities. Love of God comes first. And love of self is a pre-condition for love of neighbour which comes second. This is the starting-point for any Christian contribution to any discussion about religion and morality or religion and politics. It warns us that it is a very grave mistake to put love of neighbour in first place - which is, of course, precisely what the good godless are condemned to doing. What happens when love of neighbour is given priority over love of God and love of self? Jesus reminds us that we are to love our neighbour as ourself. Perhaps we have the idea that it is wrong to love ourself. Are self-love and selfishness not the same thing? But how are we to love our neighbour if we do not love first ourself in an appropriate way?

Perhaps we have had the experience of being loved by someone who did not love themself. Perhaps we have had the experience of being loved by someone who hated themself. It is not a pleasant experience. It is a hurtful and damaging experience - because there are no neutral relationships between people. Every relationship between people is for better or for worse. Every relation- ship either helps or harms the people involved. So if I hate myself it just will not do to launch into loving my neighbour as myself. If I do that I will certainly cause harm and havoc.

So I am to begin by loving myself. Not of course the obvious kind of self-love that is the essence of sin. Not the kind of self-adoration that makes me my own god. Our spiritual journey starts off from there. Perhaps our experience of hurting and dam- aging those we make the focus of our selfish love is what encourages us to begin the journey. Through our fail- ure to love others we come to hate all sin and selfishness in ourselves and it is then that the image of God in us begins to emerge. That image of love that God himself loves in us and that alone we are to love in one another.

You must love the Lord your God with all your heart, with all your soul, and with all your mind. This is the greatest and the first commandment. Those who love God are at peace with themselves and love their neighbour in a helpful, wholesome and healing way. They are a long way away from all those sinful, perverted loves that warp our lives and enslave us.

Exodus 22:20-26 / First Thessalonians 1:5-10 / Matthew 22:34-40

Thirty-First Sunday

You are all brothers…. The greatest among you must be your servant.

A challenging gospel this, brothers and sisters in Christ, when we ask about our actual experience of the various little worlds in which we live and move and have our being. You have only one master, and you are all brothers and sisters. The greatest among you must be your servant. Anyone who exalts himself will be humbled. This is a Gospel of equality, respect and love. It abolishes all and every distinction between one human being and another. We all owe our ultimate allegiance, loyalty and obedience to God our Father in heaven. Because God is our Father we are all members of the one human family: every other human being is our brother or sister - and there are no exceptions, however much we might squirm at the thought.

We are all brothers and sisters: is this not the deepest lesson of our Christian faith? For this brotherhood, this awareness that we all belong to the

one family of God is not a vague
feeling of being well disposed
towards others within well defined
limits. The reality of it is in fact a
sign, indeed a proof, that there really
is a God who is the loving Father of
us all. The living bond of love that
gathers us together into the brotherhood of the Church is in the end the
only convincing indication that Jesus
is truly risen from the dead and that
he has triumphed on our behalf over
all that introduces hatred and divis-
ion into the human world

At the very beginning of that Church
it was this striking brotherliness of
the first Christian communities that
attracted converts and drew the curiosity of the pagan world. They were
a light in the darkness. Those who
saw their lives were filled with an
irresistible curiosity to know their
secret. What was the source of this
love that Christians had for one
another? What was the basis for their
extraordinary solidarity? And what
did the genuine inquirer find if not
their living faith in Jesus Christ, their
faith in Jesus who had died for them
on the cross to show them how to

live and was risen from the dead to offer them the sure hope of eternal life with God?

How many converts can we count today? How many of us are committed to our own ongoing conversion? When did it last occur to us that now might be the time to begin to take it all seriously, to wake up to God and to look for the Christ in those around us? If the Church as we know it today does not always seem to us to be on fire with this striking sense of brotherhood and unity and solidarity that so success-fully advertised it at its beginning what is to be done? To remember these challenging and provocative words of Jesus is to begin to make the fresh start that is needed: You have only one Father, and he is in heaven. You have only one master, and you are all brothers and sisters. The greatest among you must be your servant.

Malachi 1:14 – 2:2.8-10 / First Thessalonians 2:7-9.13 / Matthew 23:1-12

Thirty-Second Sunday

At midnight there was a cry: The Bridegroom is here! Go out and meet him.

The message of today's parable is familiar enough, brothers and sisters in Christ. We are not to take life for granted. We have no guarantee that we will still be here this evening. Death often comes as a surprise: we are too young or we are in the prime of life or we have lived so long that we have forgotten about it. Today Jesus invites us urgently: Stay awake, because you do not know either the day or the hour.

We might want to open our eyes and look at where our lives are going and perhaps ask ourselves a few hard questions. None of the bridesmaids were so foolish as to forget their lamps - but the sensible ones made sure to take some extra oil with them. Few of us are so foolish as to abandon the practice of our religion altogether. We come to Mass on Sundays and if pressed we admit to being Catholics. But that might seem a bit reckless. It could be sensible to do something more.

The sensible believer will realize that it is an all-or-nothing situation. Too little is no use at all. And later is always too late. If our faith is not the central core of our lives the lamp of our soul is being starved of oil and sooner or later it will splutter and go out. Often we are too like the foolish bridesmaids for comfort. They might as well have stayed at home.

At midnight there was a cry. The Bridegroom is here! Go out to meet him. These words that spelt such joy for the sensible bridesmaids and such confusion for their foolish company-ions remind us that we too will be called, just as we are, at a moment we least expect, to answer for the use we have made of the life that has been given us, to answer for the gifts, the graces, the blessings, the chal-lenges and above all the time, the days, the hours and the minutes that have been ours and that we have used to make of ourselves - for better or for worse - what we now are. We will be called just as we are, at a moment we least expect.

So this parable is a timely warning. The sceptic will doubt whether it will make any difference to the sad endings of the stories of the foolish and the careless. We all get stubborn and set in our ways. But God does not give up on us. He prods us and prompts us. His wisdom pursues us. The parables of Jesus are part of his strategy. On other occasions the message is the comforting one that there is still time, it is not yet too late. Here the emphasis is on the urgency of it all. The last minutes before midnight are ticking away and last minute conversions are as sensible as any. The foolish had gone off to buy oil just when the bridegroom arrived. Those who were ready went into the wedding hall and the door was closed.

We all dream about changes we'd like to make in the way we live. Let's make those changes now, today, before it really is too late.

Sundays in Ordinary Time – Year A

Wisdom 6:12-16 / First Thessalonians 4:13-18 / Matthew 25:1-13

Thirty-Third Sunday

"Well done, good and faithful servant; you have shown you can be faithful in small things..... Come and join in your master's happiness".

This parable of the talents, brothers and sisters in Christ, is meant to teach us something about how we are to spend our time while we are waiting for our Lord to come again. We proclaim your death, O Lord, and profess your resurrection until you come again. We are familiar with these words. They are words we use to express our response to the mystery of God's love for us. Jesus died on the cross to save us from our sins. He rose from the dead so that we might share his new life. This is his gift to us, his invitation to follow him along the path he himself has traced out for us, the path that will lead us through our own cross to resurrection with him.

We proclaim your death, O Lord, and profess your resurrection until you come again. Even the finest words can become empty and hollow, until we no longer even hear ourselves saying them. We proclaim your death, O Lord: but perhaps it was just another death, another violent and ugly death, almost two thousand years ago, no different from millions of other similar deaths. I can so easily forget in the turmoil of my life that Christ died for me.

We profess your resurrection: but perhaps this is just another pious fantasy to shelter us from the finality of death. I can so easily forget in the routine of my days that Christ rose from the dead so that my life would be different.

We proclaim your death, O Lord, and profess your resurrection until you come again. Is this return of our Lord really the expectation that structures our lives as Christians? When Jesus does come a second time I need not think that I will be able to hide in the crowd. He will be asking to see me. Will I have to appear before him, still trembling from my fevered attempt to unearth at last the gift of life so deeply and despairingly buried a lifetime before in a place I had all but forgotten? Will I say to him, "Here it is, Lord. It was yours. You have it back"? What reply could I expect from him when I have already pronounced sentence upon myself?

The mercy of this seemingly harsh parable is that my story can have a happy ending: I can today let go of my bitterness that life seems to have dealt others a better hand. I can begin to see that my one talent can be all to me that their two or five or ten is to them. I can gently unearth it. I can courageously risk it in a new commitment to the ordinary demands of everyday life. That is what it means to await the blessed hope and the coming of our Saviour Jesus Christ. I will not then have to prepare a speech for our meeting. He will simply say to me, "Well done, good and faithful servant. You have been faithful in small things. Come and join in your master's happiness".

Proverbs 31:10-13.19-20.30-31 / First Thessalonians 5:1-6 / Matthew 25:14-30

Printed in Great Britain
by Amazon